Chocolate Bella

by Sukenya Best

A visual depiction of a tour to Florence, Rome and Paris

Written by
Sukenya I. Best

Cover and artwork by
Sukenya I. Best

Editor
Rebekah L. Pierce
editor@averagegirlmagazine.com

Chocolate Bella. Copyright © 2013 by Sukenya Best. All rights reserved. Printed in the United States of America. No part of this book may be used or reproduced in any form or by any electronic or mechanical means including information storage and retrieval systems without written permission of the publisher or copyright owner.
All rights reserved.
ISBN: 978-0-615-88120-1

This book is in Memory of Alfred Goode Jr., Program Assistant for Virginia Union University's Center for International Studies. The current director of the center is Dr. David Adewuyi.

In the summer of 2012 (June 15-22), I had the pleasure of taking an eight day educational tour to Rome and Florence, Italy as well as Paris, France. Mr. Goode organized and coordinated the trip through Education First College Study Tour (EF Tours). The group was made up of two faculty, one staff and eight VUU students. Dr. David Adewuyi revealed that this was the first trip of its kind since the University's birth in 1865.

This book of cartoons captures day to day moments of the group's visit to various sites in the two cities in Italy and Paris, France. I enjoyed drawing and coloring actual faculty, students, tour guides and the various places. It is my hope that this book of cartoons inspires you to travel abroad.

Enjoy!

Sukenya Best

Ellie walks ahead of us as we walk casually to the Piazza Navona led by EF tour guide, Matteo. This is our first day in Rome, and so I imagine a written path leading us to the heart of Rome.

In good company, Dria and Katrina anticipate seeing the Four Rivers Fountain, the church of St. Agnes and the Pantheon.

Our goal is to not get lost, so Alfred talks to Matteo about navigating through the heart of Rome. Naturally, our first interest is to change our U.S. dollars into Euros and eat authentic Italian food.

I delight in seeing the many artists, art vendors, outdoor cafes and tasting flavorful gelato. One of the vendors holds up a printed reproduction of the Colosseum.

This art vendor bears a shocking resemblance to Albert Einstein and Mark Twain. In front of the church of St. Agnes, he hangs up his posters and prances around in his slippers.

For three straight mornings, we chow down on breakfast on the roof of the Carlo Mango Hotel. Roommates Dria & Faustina are fueling themselves up for our walk through the Colosseum, Roman Forum, Spanish Steps and the Trevi Fountain.

Across the Tiber River in the area known as Trastevere City, Kyerra and Shanice converse with Dr. Adewuyi about lunch. The church of Santa Maria is nearby; it features a fountain that is said to date back to the 8th century.

Learning about the history of Italy from the Vatican City tour guide, Carla, was an amazing experience. We stop at the end of the Map Gallery to hear how the obelisks traveled from Egypt to Rome. The painting, "Civita Vetus," was the source of this topic of conversation.

Here, you witness Faustina's epiphany in the Vatican City Museum. We are in one of Raphael's Rooms before going to the Sistine Chapel. We continue to marvel at the ceiling painting, "Triumph of Christianity," and gawk at the painting, "School of Athens."

In Vatican City, we enter St. Peter's Basilica, which covers 6 acres and can hold 60,000 visitors. The church is named after one of Jesus' disciples who was crucified here in A.D. 65. Faustina and I are at one of the two holy water fountains. Visitors can still follow the ritual of cleansing themselves at the fountain.

The Colosseum tour guide speaks about bloody battles between gladiators and caged animals in the arena's underground passageway. This was Rome's most popular place for entertainment in A.D. 80.

Fashionable Halley from California is a clean contrast to the 1/3 of the Colosseum that remains standing today. Before destruction, the oval shaped arena was 280 ft. long by 165 ft. wide; in Ancient Greece, the 5 to 3 ratio was a mathematically spiritual philosophy that symbolized the essence of life.

In Florence, the tour through the courtyard of Palazzo Vecchio is invigorating. The palace has a 308 ft. bell tower (Giotto's Campanile). We also saw a 200 year old copy of Michelangelo's sculpture of David.

That's right! Pinocchio (1881-present) is Italian. Well, his creator was! I'm not talking about Geppetto the carpenter, but Carlo Collodi, the writer of the famous story. As a matter of fact, he was from Tuscany. Florence is its capital city.

You know you have genuine leather when you look at the lining and it says "made in Italy" in gold leaf. Leather has been important to Florence since the Middle Ages. At this demonstration, Ellie is listening closely to the traditional methods of cutting, shaping and firing leather.

The Louvre in Paris, France is home to over 30,000 pieces of artwork. The five level 652,300 square ft. museum is the most visited museum in the world. Here I am on the ground floor of the museum, embodying the Greek statue of Posedion's wife, Amphitrite with their son Triton.

Matteo is talking to a couple of tourists from California in Paris, France. They are standing across from the building, Les Invalides, which has housed the burial tomb of Napoleon 1 since 1861.

I have attached myself to this military statue, not too far from the Californian tourists. Les Invalides, which is across the street, is both a military museum and a retirement home for war veterans.

Faustina and Dria are sitting in the park below the Eiffel Tower. On this sunny day, they see lovers, tight rope walkers and children playing tag in the park. Just ten minutes earlier, we had climbed the 1,000 ft-tall monument, which is over 600 steps. Inside, there are two high class restaurants, souvenir stores, restrooms and an elevator. The tower has also operated as a radio transmitter since 1909.

We end our trip in Paris, France. Here, a stranger passes us along the Seine River. There are 32 bridges over the river, and the ones that we cross are covered with the locks of lovers from all over the world.

Sukenya Best is a native New Yorker who moved to Richmond, Virginia with her family in 1989. Richmond has been her home for over 20 years. She is an alumnus from Virginia Commonwealth University (VCU), Department of Painting and Printmaking, having received a Bachelor of Fine Arts in 2001. During her studies at VCU, she also studied abroad in Europe and Africa. In 2007, she received a Master of Fine Arts Degree from the University of Tennessee, Knoxville (UTK). There, she studied in the Printmaking Program (ranked #3 nationally).

Internationally, Sukenya's artwork is in the collection of New Delhi and Gujarat, India. In the states, exhibitions have taken place at the Museutm of Science & Industry (Chicago), Pen & Brush Inc. (New York), Pittsburgh Center for the Arts (Pennsylvania), Kansas City Art Institute (Missouri), Corcoran School of Arts (Washington, D.C.) and the Cultural Arts Center at Glen Allen (Virginia). In the spring of 2008, she was featured in the international publication of *Studio Visit Magazine*, and in the summer of 2013, she was honored by Richmond's *Style Weekly*, "Women in the Arts."

Sukenya has worked in multiple areas with professional artists such as: Whitfield Lovell, Millicent Johnnie, Roger Shimomura, John Newman, Beauvais Lyons and Anita Jung. She has also collaborated with Circle Modern Dance Company (Knoxville, TN), and worked with the Latin Ballet of Virginia (Richmond, VA).

Currently, Sukenya is a full-time instructor at Virginia Union University and an Assistant Professor at Reynolds Community College (summers) where she teaches courses in drawing, painting, printmaking and design. She also continues to create and exhibit art from her world travels.

www.ingramcontent.com/pod-product-compliance
Lightning Source LLC
Chambersburg PA
CBHW042035150426
43201CB00002B/33